AWAKEN YOUR INNER LION

TOLU' A. AKINYEMI

First published in Great Britain as a softback original in 2022

Design by Buzzdesignz

Published by The Roaring Lion Newcastle LTD.

ISBN: 978-1-913636-36-4
eISBN: 978-1-913636-37-1

Email:
tolu@toluakinyemi.com
author@tolutoludo.com

Website:
www.toluakinyemi.com
www.tolutoludo.com

Dedication

To God Almighty

and

Everyone who has supported me on my journey to becoming.

CONTENTS

CONTENTS

Acknowledgements

Sincere appreciation to my partner, Olabisi, for the incredible support on my author journey.

A special word of thanks to my exceptional children, Isaac and Abigail Akinyemi, I do not take your support and constant encouragement for granted.

I'm eternally indebted to my parents, Gabriel and Temidayo Akinyemi, for nurturing me with life-long teachings and skills that have greatly prepared me for life.

I'm also thankful for friends and family who have supported me on this booktiful journey that has turned out to be a phenomenal success.

Lastly, I'd like to say thank you to my editors, Diane Donovan and Adeola Gbalajobi. It was nice working with you on this project.

CHAPTER 1

ON A MISSION

'Starting with an end in mind means we are not tossed 'to' and 'fro' by every wind or storm.'
– Tolu' A. Akinyemi

Growing up, I was always fascinated when I saw people walking in different directions. This shows the multiplicity of missions in life. However, the sad thing is, many people wander on earth with no sense of vision and mission. These are the people who become inconsequential in the grand scheme of things.

There are times when we don't have a vivid picture of what our mission will be. That is where having a life vision becomes important, as our life's vision helps us shape our mission and make it come alive. Our vision is the driving force behind the totality of our existence. It's the reason we live, while our mission is the engine that drives the fulfilment of that vision.

A vision statement helps us to envision our future. It helps us think about it, plan for it, and take practical steps to achieve the dream.

Can you imagine driving a car with both eyes closed? It sounds ludicrous and reckless, right? Well, such is living a life that has no vision, leaving your life to chance and happenstance.

As a writer, I had a vision of winning literary awards. That vision has come to fruition today because I had a plan of action.

What is your life vision? What is your mission?

In my career, excellence is the bedrock of all I do. And this has led to winning awards in the workplace and getting recognition for making invaluable contributions to overall corporate objectives.

Today, I'm a mentor to young writers because I have built competency over the years. Without such competencies, I wouldn't have been able to support others—an empty cistern cannot quench thirst. What helped me remain committed to building myself is the vision I have, which is followed by actions.

This applies to you, too. Whatever you'll become in years to come starts with a vision and the efforts you put into bringing the vision to life. You must be committed to your life's vision and mission.

Below are some tips to energise us on the mission ahead:

Be Focused

A person on a mission is always focused on the journey ahead. When sent on a mission, a soldier never loses his focus. He avoids distractions and commits himself fully to the mission before him. You should approach your mission with this same level of focus and discipline. Avoid distractions and being too involved in things that are not part of your vision.

Keeping in mind that your input to your mission determines your output in life will help you stay focused on your mission. Whenever I'm driving to a new location, I use my car's satellite navigation system to find my way. Any time I lose my focus and take my eyes off the navigation system, I miss the correct turn, and then I have to either turn back or find a new route, which costs me time.

Whenever we are on a mission and we lose focus (like I occasionally do at the steering wheel), then we need to re-route and correct our error so we can arrive at the right destination.

One area in which I have always tried my best to maintain clear focus is on the road. I have never had a speeding ticket issued against me since I started driving in the United Kingdom. I see driving as a mission that involves focusing and maintaining the right speed and momentum.

You can maintain a high level of focus in every area of your life. To achieve the right outcomes in your life, career, and relationships, be focused and let your drive for excellence help you achieve the seemingly impossible.

That you're holding this book is proof that whenever I set my mind on a goal, I go all out to achieve it. You can also be on a mission with your eyes set on the goal no matter the obstacles in your way. Write the vision, make it plain, and don't relent until your goals become a reality.

Be a Self-Starter

Since the beginning of the Coronavirus pandemic, there has been a steady increase in the number of remote opportunities now available globally. However, to work in global teams remotely, one must be a self-starter.

Being a self-starter means you do not have to be pushed before you contribute to your team's objective and the overall corporate goal. It means that you're self-motivated.

Being a self-starter, being self-motivated, is a major prerequisite to navigating life's hail and storms. There will be times when life seems to be against you; times when you're alone with no one to motivate you and steer you to action. This is when you turn towards your inner strength to motivate and push yourself.

To make your life's vision and mission come to fruition, you must be proactive, ready to push, and show a determination to put in the work.

It's also not enough to have a plan of action and write down your goals. You must also show the willingness to learn, relearn, and unlearn. The ability to unlearn old habits and patterns, and learn and relearn new ones, will help you thrive in life.

If you don't need anyone to motivate you before you eat, then you don't need anyone to push you to feed your life's goals, vision, and mission. Be proactive. Be your own cheerleader. Dare to do the impossible. There is so much you can do, but you need to get up and start.

To achieve anything worthwhile in life, push yourself when no one is there to push and encourage you.

Every morning, I wake up, put on my running shoes, and I run approximately five miles. This has been my morning routine for over fourteen years. After ten years of consistent running, I no longer need anyone to push me to go for my morning run. I know that being in good physical health and in shape boosts my mental agility, and so I keep to it, motivating myself to run every day, rain or shine.

Start with an End in Mind

Always have the end in mind when starting a new pursuit. Why is this important? There are times when our minds are unable to conceive the full picture. What then keeps us in line with a sense of purpose is the end that we have in mind.

For example, I intend to publish this book by the third quarter of the year. Questions such as when am I likely to complete the first draft will help me gauge if I am going in the right direction.

Also, having an end goal in mind means that we are not embarking on an immeasurable and fruitless mission. If there are no project objectives, how do we measure the milestones and celebrate those little successes? Hence, starting a mission with the end in mind also serves as a tool for measuring our progress.

As a student who is focused on achieving A's in GCSEs or A-Levels exams, having the foreknowledge that your success will be due to your preparedness will help you put all your efforts into it.

Not having an end goal in mind means that we are prone to becoming like people who are products of life's circumstances who hinge their success on some sort of luck or fortune.

Having an end goal is a 'must-have' in our toolkit for a successful mission.

Be Prepared

On a recent road trip from the North-East of England to the North-West, I checked my tyres and my oil, filled up my tank with diesel, ensured that my wiper blades were in good condition, and saw that I had enough screen washer to clean the windscreens. All these measures were to ensure that the journey was as smooth as it could be. That's the essence of preparation.

Are you alive in the place of preparation? To have a successful life mission and vision, we must not be asleep in the place of preparation. To achieve success in every facet of life, adequate preparation is required. It is what separates winners from losers. To achieve your goals, you must be awake in the place of preparation. Preparation means that you do not leave your life to timing and chance. Being prepared means you're ready to show up in the audition of life, always putting your best foot forward.

I have sat for and passed many professional exams during my career's journey. And to achieve the mission of 'first-time pass' means that I do not laze in the place of preparation.

Many times, people envy your result. They want the product, but want to bypass the process. The fine ornaments that sparkle which we covet because they ooze class have gone through pruning before they become a representation of class and beauty.

Preparation is the process that births the result. If you desire the result, never bypass the process. Own the mission and show up in style. Life rewards people who are committed to the process. Quit making excuses and get your hands on the plough.

Invest your time in preparation for your life's goal. We have one life to live, and it behoves us to give it our best shot. Life will not be fair to you if you do nothing. On my writing journey, I have been able to publish many books because adequate preparation is something that I value. For those who are prepared, when the opportunities come, they can leverage them. A lot of times, our opportunities come when we are least prepared for them, and these opportunities which could occur only once in a lifetime pass us by because we are not ready for them.

As a mentor to many writers, I know writers who are passionate about the art of writing and are always prepared to leverage the opportunities presented to them, while there are others who are neither invested in their art nor prepared to leverage opportunities.

Preparation shows how much you want something. In the financial crime compliance space, I can change jobs at will because I have not tarried in the place of preparation.

In my undergraduate days in southwestern Nigeria, to prepare for our exams we would read with lanterns and candles because constant electricity blackouts were a problem. Back in those days, how well I was prepared for my exams always showed in my grades. This has taught me some things in life: that the result you get is in direct proportion to how well you prepared.

*****

As I round up this chapter, I must balance my thoughts. I understand that life can sometimes be unpredictable, and that time and chance determine a lot of things. However, it's those who are prepared who can take advantage of time and chance.

Also, I know that having a grand vision and mission may be too much to ask of those who are just striving to survive present storms, but there is the need to project beyond the present storm and know that no matter how tough it is, it'll pass. This mindset has been my anchor when I'm wading through my storms.

The things we do every day—those little steps we take towards the achievement of our vision—are what culminate in success.

I envision a life where I will someday retire from my career in the financial services sector and live off my writing. Whether I get to achieve this depends on some of the factors I have listed above.

I'm a man on a mission. A mission to achieve extraordinary results as a writer. By keeping a clear focus, having the end in mind, and not lazing in the place of preparation, I'll surely achieve this.

Do not be deterred if your present life does not look like the desired end. Keep trudging on, keep the vision alive, write it down, measure it, own it, and take responsibility for the achievement of your life's outcomes.

This is your mission, and you're in it to win.

CHAPTER 2

CULTIVATING HEALTHY RELATIONSHIPS

'Relationships are like gardens, with flowers and weeds fighting for territorial dominance.'

– Tolu' A. Akinyemi

For anyone to go far in life and for them to become successful, they must have the right relationship. I have seen men of little means become influential figures in society because they are in the right circle. Rightly put, they mingled with the right set of people. Then, there are people who failed to achieve anything meaningful in life because of their ego and pride. Some have made a shipwreck of their life because of being in the wrong circle.

Many times, we wallow in ignorance and suffer the consequences of our lack of knowledge. I have seen people who were at the lower cadre of the economic rung because they could not see beyond the present. Until they make the move or change friends, they never arrive at their dream destination. Relationships are like gardens, with flowers and weeds fighting for territorial dominance. You must be deliberate about getting rid of the weeds.

Are you able to spot a parasitic relationship? Those are the friends who are in the habit of taking from you without any commensurate contributions to your life. Do you know what true friendship is all about? Can you spot a fake friend when you see one? What signs do you look for, to see if that person in your life is a true friend or a parasite that needs to be removed?

Harsh as it might sound, I have people I no longer respond to because they have become parasites. They're always asking for one favour or another, yet they bring no valuable addition to our relationship. I have become wary of such people and I tend to discontinue such relationships when these patterns are noticed.

You must be intentional about who you allow into your life. Remember that an unhealthy relationship is like a virus that can damage body cells. Before you call somebody your friend, ask yourself: what value are they bringing to the table? Value doesn't always have to be money or gifts. It could be in the little things like sincerity of purpose, acts of kindness, love, honesty, and the gestures that money cannot buy.

As an author with influence and connections, I have known writers who I have provided with ample opportunities for events, interview features, and wider publicity; but despite this, they, on the other hand, always kept their own opportunities to themselves. When you're in a relationship with people who only want to leverage your network but are not willing to do the same for you, then you have to be wary of such friendships.

You do not have to be friends with everyone. Also, some relationships belong to the past. Leave it where it belongs—the past. Many of my close allies from my early school days are no longer my friends. Life has happened and we have all moved on. It's not your duty to flog a dead horse back to life. Not everyone will be lifelong friends or will make that transition to the next phase with you. We must understand that life happens in phases, and there are times and seasons even to our relationships. Hence, there are friendships that won't be part of our next chapter, and that's okay, too.

If your close circles are into substance abuse, gang wars, or internet fraud, that is a bold sign of a cancerous relationship. There are times when the handwriting is crystal clear. All we need to do is weed out those relationships that can cause us harm.

In friendships, learn to set healthy boundaries so that all the parties involved know their limits, draw back when they overstep their bounds, and know what the other person likes or dislikes.

Also, if a relationship isn't working, it might be appropriate to take a step back and re-evaluate if the relationship is worth keeping or investing in.

As a mentor to aspiring writers, I have encountered mentees who eventually became burdens too difficult to manage. They burden their mentors with unnecessary financial responsibility, or they transfer their family issues to him or her without pausing to think that the mentor also has a life to live.

Yes, a mentor can help, but the purpose of mentorship isn't to bear others' responsibilities. It is simply to guide you through a shared area of interest.

This is why it is important to set clear expectations of such relationships from the onset.

Setting healthy boundaries means that no one is taking advantage of the other. A relationship becomes strained when one party begins to see the other as a burden.

Showing a high level of integrity is one of the ways to cultivate healthy relationships. The value of integrity in cultivating healthy relationships should never be underestimated. Lack of integrity can ruin a relationship.

I have a mentee who would always spend money given to him to execute projects on personal frivolities. Then he'd come back with one story or another, of how he had used the money given to him for a business, or to settle a personal matter. Even though I took no offence and would give him time to make it good, I knew this was someone who had issues with financial integrity, and I was ready for the worst whenever I gave him money.

******

I once helped three colleagues secure a new role at a Global Investment Bank when we all got disillusioned with our jobs at a retail bank due to lack of direction and clarity of purpose on the project. Our former colleague (who was at the new workplace) became bitter that I helped some people secure a job at his workplace. Instead of taking up the issue with me, he went to discuss it with another colleague, instead. He was cold to me when I reached out to enquire about the culture of his workplace.

Once I found out the reason for his coldness towards me, I knew it was time to end our relationship. Why are you bitter because I helped someone secure a job? Why didn't you reach out to me instead of allowing bitterness to take you over?

When cultivating healthy relationships, eliminate entitlement mentality. My partner used to say something that resonates with me all the time: *If you're not calling or texting that person in your life, do not take offence when they have not called you, either. If you have not heard from someone you love and care about, pick up the phone and reach out to them.*

This is a sure way to save a relationship from ending—by being committed to communication.

Don't make assumptions about people and their situations. I remember when my family was down with Covid-19 and I was ill and out of touch with friends, at the time. It would have been unfair if anyone had taken offence for me not reaching out to them during this period, for they didn't know what I was going through.

I have also been guilty of making assumptions about people, in the past. But, through self-awareness and evaluation, I realised how wrong this was, and I made the necessary correction. Being self-aware and considerate of the feelings of others is important for building relationships that will stand the test of time.

In 2021, I exited my high school's alumni WhatsApp group because an alumnus had raised a call to action to support a needy person. However, because people did not respond in time, she resorted to throwing tantrums, making assumptions without considering that they might have been engaged with their issues. I gave her a piece of my mind and exited the group.

Not About You

Relationships should not be about you alone. I had a close family member who became angry and bitter because they think their friends should make an enemy of their enemy.

For context: they had portrayed to the family that someone was an evil person so that they could become close with new family members. However, this tactic failed woefully when new members of the family gradually became friends with the 'bad girl'. They, on the other hand, then made an enemy of everybody because they didn't join them in their campaign of hatred against the person, as if the family and relationships revolved around them alone.

People like to have friends around them who caress and massage their egos. However, in building healthy relationships, we need to maintain a balance by having people in our lives who are not afraid to tell us the truth when we err, or who keep us in check to ensure we do not go astray.

Also, to have healthy relationships, we must be willing to practice self-denial and avoid selfishness. Selfishness is what ends many relationships when one party wants things to go their way all the time.

Cultivating healthy relationships means we will have to be ready to forgive and not take revenge when we're offended. There will be days when we need to turn the other cheek or reach a compromise in order for peace to reign.

Are You Emotionally Intelligent?

Emotional Intelligence is a tool that we need to always deploy. Growing up, my parents taught us what native intelligence (or common sense) is, and through their body language, we understood their unspoken words. Being emotionally intelligent is a sure way to sustain our relationships. Maturity is not about age, but how emotionally intelligent we are—how we deal with complex issues and situations that arise in our relationships.

I once had to settle a conflict between some friends. I went to Party A to speak to them and reduce the tension in the air. I admonished Party A not to always speak ill of Party C to Party B. She said she would heed to my words. She, however, went ahead to accuse Party B of leaking what she'd said about Party C, repeating what I said to the other party. This action showed that they lack native intelligence.

This is why I mentioned, earlier, that sustaining or building relationships should not always be about you or your ego. Having people pandering to you or massaging your ego should not always be what gives you joy.

Can you accept negative feedback? As a financial crime compliance consultant with Quality Control and Assurance experience, giving and receiving feedback has been a major part of my career journey. So, I understand that feedback is not about the giver or receiver but about ensuring that we reach fair outcomes for all the parties involved.

Understand Human Nature

In recent years, I have gained insight into people and their characters. This has helped me to lower my expectations in terms of character traits and behavioural expectations. My attitude these days is: 'To whom much is given, less is expected.' This is not about expecting less from others, but by understanding the nature of humans to quickly forget where they are coming from, you do not easily take offence or get disappointed.

As an example, I have had people who, when looking for favours, behaved as if they were respectful people with impeccable characters. However, once they got what they wanted, they showed what they were really made of.

As humans, we are prone to making mistakes, forgetting, and returning evil for good. Understanding this sad fact of human frailty will help you avoid disappointments. It will also help you to do good not just for the rewards that come from such actions, but to extend goodness without expectations. This will give you peace of mind.

*****

Cultivating healthy relationships is a recipe for a happy life. Just as toxic relationships are the cause of bitterness and strife, healthy relationships improve our health and wellbeing. Our relationships affect our mental and emotional health.

Also, we must be brave enough to leave unhealthy relationships. If you're in an emotionally abusive or violent relationship, don't stay, hoping to change the person and turn the relationship into a healthy one. Many have tried to do this, and sadly, they paid dearly for it.

When a relationship is not working as it should be, communicate your grievance to the other person. Relationships deteriorate when hurts and offences are not addressed.

I was in a relationship with someone who always wanted to have the last say on every issue. They could not control their emotions when they were hurt either in private or public. Our relationship became toxic and unhealthy. However, by discussing the issues affecting our relationship, we were able to resolve those differences, and today we have a far better relationship.

In healthy relationships, you do not always have to have the last word. Cultivating healthy relationships means there will be times you have to put your interests aside for the greater good. Also, having open and honest conversations can help to reduce tensions in a relationship. When you spot an issue, address it before it snowballs into a bigger one.

Communication is the bedrock of healthy relationships, and lack of communication means we are most likely going to misunderstand each other. Lack of communication leads to bigger issues like malice, deep-seated wounds, and ill feelings.

Another invaluable virtue that can help us to cultivate healthy relationships is listening. Before you react, ask yourself if you are listening or have listened enough to understand the problem. When we listen to issues or concerns, this helps us to understand the root cause, and work towards a resolution.

Lastly, remember that how far you'll go in life and how well you'll end up depend on the kind of relationships you have.

CHAPTER 3

THE SLIPPERY SLOPE

'When the family fails, society falls on its head.'
– Tolu' A. Akinyemi

The world we live in today is different from the one I grew up in. Life wasn't a Nirvana then, but we were ingrained with virtues like discipline, respect, and the dignity of labour from home. There was a sense of community and people looked out for one another. We've lost these things.

For all the good it has brought, civilisation seems to be driving humanity into a pit of lawlessness. Society as we have it today is on a downward spiral. We have lost it all: our humanity, values, sense of community, love, peace, and a united home front. For some of us who grew up when the home was tightly knit, the reality of things today is a constant shock to us.

Today, woke culture has turned everything on its head. As popular culture evolves, society becomes a decrepit hut. As we evolve, the bastion of society becomes weaker. Unchecked liberal ideology has led to an erosion of sound judgement. Age-long traditions that have been the mainstay of many communities around the world are being done away with. People pant for freedom, but what we have now is an implosion of lawlessness right in our faces.

There are no longer values like respect, love, and peace in homes. Ill-mannered children who later become a menace to society are being raised. The Tottenham riots (widely known as the 2011 England riots) come to mind. Many high street shops were looted and burnt across the city following the death of Mark Duggan, a local man who was shot dead by the police. The way the riots imploded shows that many youths either had no parents who could call them to order, or they were simply above reprimand. As good values crumble and lawlessness triumphs on our streets, the aftermath is that many bright stars were sentenced to jail for issues that should never have occurred if not for dysfunction at home and in society. In the long run, a jail sentence does more harm than good to society, as jailbirds are likely to come back to haunt their communities by descending further into a life of crime.

In order for society to function properly, the family unit has a pivotal role to play in helping us keep it all together.

As parents, we have to correct our children when they fall out of line. Cuddle them when they need cuddling, but never be afraid to tell them the truth when it needs telling. Covering up inappropriate behaviour sends society on a descent into chaos.

People like me, who thirst for knowledge and are breaking ground in their various fields, are not celebrated enough. The algorithm on social media does not favour the intellectual. Instead, it drives traffic to the pages of people who are corrupting our children—people who should be held up as bad examples, by a sane society.

Sex is no longer about spending an intimate moment with a loved one or sexual partner. As seen in recent examples of the leaked sex tapes of Nigerian music stars Tiwa Savage and Oxlade on Twitter, sex sells, and has become accessible more than ever before. The problem of the easy availability of sex means that virtue is no longer talked about as much as pornography is shoved down our throats on television ads, music videos, social media platforms, and many other online channels. We have normalised impropriety in the name of providing content for our followers. People are more inclined to attempt the bizarre as we descend into this slope where honour and values have become relegated.

Knife crimes and gang wars have been a plague in London. And this exposes how the family unit has deteriorated. When the family fails, society inadvertently falls apart. The incessant stabbings in London and its metropolis show a deep-rooted problem that would take systemic and urgent actions to stop. Why is a life of crime so appealing to young people? How have young people become so vile that they thirst for blood and seek to extinguish the light in others? How do we rescue our young people from this cesspool? Answering these questions would be the first step in finding a lasting solution to a problem that has defied political solutions.

Any solution that excludes the role of the family in re-orientating young people would fail. Noble as the intention of government might be, the family has a more important role to play in fixing the youth.

The United States of America continues to deal with gun violence and school shootings, which occur at an alarming rate. We have buried too many of our young, and their night's song became dirges just after daybreak. Our minds have been trained to get used to violence, such that on platforms like TikTok, people pretend to be shooting down schools, making parents scared to let their children leave home for school the next day. The rate at which that kind of social media challenge went viral shows how broken our society is. On this disaster plane, violence has been normalised and the solution to these problems evades us all.

****

Abba Kyari, a celebrated super-cop in Nigeria who received a medal of courage from the President in 2016 after his team rescued three kidnapped schoolgirls in Lagos (and was also honoured by the House of Representatives), was recently arrested by the Nigeria Police Force after a sting operation on him (conducted by the National Drug Law Enforcement Agency) led the NDLEA to declare him wanted. He was accused of "being a member of a drug cartel that operates the Brazil-Ethiopia-Nigeria illicit drug pipeline." The suspended super-cop was also facing extradition to the United States of America for allegedly helping internet fraudster Hushpuppi launder money. The above example shows how much rot is in society. When law enforcement officers aid and albeit the same criminals they are supposed to rid the society of, then our freefall into the mire becomes imminent.

In the United Kingdom, the police watchdog The Independent Office for Police Conduct (IOPC), during their investigation of the Charring Cross Station Case, indicted metropolitan officers who joked about raping women, flaying the culture of fear prevalent within the metropolitan police force. The messages sent via text and WhatsApp messages by members of the police force showed a culture of misogyny, sexism, racism, bullying, homophobia, and repugnant beliefs held by members of the metropolitan police. The alarming rot within the police force shows the deep rot within an institution that ought to uphold law and justice in society.

The radicalization and indoctrination of people (especially young people) into terrorist organisations are new lows of the slippery slope that society is descending onto. I have seen gory sights that would terrify even the strongest of men. Society as we have it today has lost more than a thread of humanity. The wickedness in the hearts of men is beyond comprehension. Many people now live in internally displaced camps while sorrow, blood, and tears colour our skies. Who will redeem humanity? Who will return us to the better place to which we were once accustomed?

Our governments are failing us by the day. While families were on lockdown in the United Kingdom, the prime minister, Boris Johnson, and his allies were on a party spree, not minding the restrictions imposed by his government and the humongous death toll that piled up by the day.

Our desires and wants are clouding our sense of judgement. COVID-19 contract scams in many countries show that we don't know where to draw the line. Many are dying and crying, while many others have become overnight multimillionaires and billionaires because of the Coronavirus pandemic, using other peoples' misfortune to enrich themselves.

Recently, an older brother couldn't correct his younger brother who'd disrespected their parents because he didn't want to hurt his brother's feelings.

I stepped in and corrected him firmly. I made him see the folly in dishonouring his parents. He saw reason and made peace with his parents.

A lot of us are like this elder brother. We are too concerned about hurting people's feelings; such that we no longer tell them the truth. What we then have is a society where people go about with frail emotions and mental strength, not able to accept and adjust to corrections because they've been pampered their whole life.

Mistakes are bound to happen in life. If God gives second chances, why do we find it so hard to give other people second chances? We are quick to judge them when they make mistakes, condemning them in the court of public opinion.

My generation has become a breeding ground for intolerant people. They can't tolerate or seek to understand the religious or ideological beliefs of other people. They're hell-bent on enforcing their worldviews on others. It's either their way or no other way.

I have seen planes brought down from the sky. I have seen humans beheading other humans, all in the name of their god. I have seen kidnappings; I have seen banditry and terrorism grow in leaps and bounds. I have cried bitter tears, seeing the terrible things that man is doing to man.

****

As the years roll by, the values and culture that should be the fundamentals of a sane society are no longer present. We have also seen the failure of leadership in the highest political offices. The insurrection at Capitol Hill on January 6, 2020 reflects the failure of political leadership in the United States. A mob of 2,000 to 2,500 supporters of former US President Donald Trump attacked the Capitol Building in Washington, D.C., seeking to overturn his defeat in the 2020 presidential election by disrupting the joint session of Congress assembled to count the electoral votes that would formalise President-elect Joe Biden's victory. The Capitol Complex was locked down, and lawmakers and staff were evacuated as rioters assaulted law enforcement officers, vandalized property, and occupied the building for several hours.

Donald Trump, who was hell-bent on staying in power despite losing the election, had repeatedly claimed that the election was rigged against him. His closest allies also amplified these lies and encouraged the January 6 attack on Capitol Hill. This shows an immense failure of political leadership, and this riot exemplifies the legacy of Donald Trump.

Public office holders elevate their interests over the public good. Free speech is no longer free, and humanity gradually loses its grips as we advance in science and technology.

With the emergence of the Coronavirus pandemic, human rights have been placed on the back burner. Even the most advanced nations who hinged their democracies on freedom for all were belaboured with incessant lockdowns and restrictions of their populace. While everyone should get the vaccine so that we can all be safe and fast-track our return to normalcy, haranguing unvaccinated people with various threats is a sign that governments no longer respect the right of citizens to make their own informed choices.

The witch-hunting of unvaccinated people, like the threat of job loss in the United Kingdom's National Health Service for unvaccinated staff members, shows that we are now in an era where leaders become tyrannical, using the machinery of government to intimidate the citizenry. The rules came into force for care home staff in November 2021, and had been due to be introduced for frontline NHS and wider social care staff in regulated settings. By April 1, 2022, NHS staff members who have not been fully jabbed risk losing their jobs. This could affect over fifty thousand NHS staff. For a health service under unimaginable pressure, which is already short-staffed, losing jobs because of not taking the vaccine is indeed a drastic action.

However, the UK government reversed its earlier decision of mandatory COVID jabs for health and social care workers in England, and the rules will be scrapped on 15 March, 2022.

In December 2021, Germany's national and regional leaders agreed to bar unvaccinated people from much of public life to fend off the fourth wave of COVID-19. Only those who have been vaccinated or recently recovered from COVID will be allowed in restaurants, cinemas, leisure facilities, and many shops. Under the measures agreed to by Germany's sixteen states and their federal leaders, unvaccinated people will be limited to meetings with their household and two other people.

In January 2022, Italy targeted the unvaccinated with a host of new coronavirus restrictions, with proof of vaccination or recovery from a recent infection required to enter public transport, cafes, hotels, gyms, and other popular venues.

These restrictions and actions from the government show that the idea of democracy has now become more theoretical than is practised. I understand the need for government to take actions that are for the greater good, even if it could be at the expense of the few, but where, then, is freedom if citizens have their movements restricted?

As someone who has been triple vaccinated and was still infected with the virus even after my third jab, I understand the need for the government's intervention to ensure that everyone is vaccinated, to curb the spread of the virus and save lives. However, making life unbearable for the unvaccinated is inhumane, and it negates their human rights and the freedom to make informed choices.

While public education and other measures put in place to encourage vaccine uptake is a great thing, a blemish on this is the lack of respect for the wishes of people who do not want to take the vaccine. The government must rethink their position and formulate policies that would not exclude these people from society.

We must build a society that is fair to everyone. And, being fair to all means that we continue to respect and value human rights. We must be able to navigate the nuances of these delicate matters.

******

Even as we descend to new lows in society, I haven't lost hope in humanity. But, for society to redeem itself, the journey to redemption has to begin in the home. What values can we pass to the upcoming generation? How do we become worthy role models to those looking up to us? The family has a pivotal role to play in ensuring that we halt this alarming descent in morality and values. It could be as simple as ingraining a message of kindness in young people and instilling values that they could strive for. If young people grow in a society where values like love, kindness, the dignity of labour and respect for others, and law and justice are instilled, we would see them grow into responsible adults.

The recent invasion of Ukraine by Russia shows that the world is now enmeshed in another needless war which has led to a major humanitarian crisis bedevilling Europe. The peace we enjoy in the world is threatened. Subtle warnings from Russian President Vladimir Putin, like ordering his nuclear deterrent forces to be on alert as international tensions over Russia's invasion of Ukraine spirals, is a major cause for concern.

The recent happenings show that nothing has changed, over the years. Have we not learnt any lessons from the war in Iraq and the fall of Afghanistan to the Taliban? We must do everything possible to ensure that we are not all drawn into another full-blown world war.

******

We mustn't allow the family to fail. Society can only be redeemed through the family unit. Ingraining the right values and providing the right leadership that children can emulate must be a fundamental part of home training to ensure that we groom responsible adults who do not become plagues on society.

Together, we can save the world by committing to doing the right thing; by evaluating our decisions and their consequences; and by promoting the principles of fairness, equality, and justice.

CHAPTER 4

YOU NEED MORE THAN DREAMS

'Successful people do not spend all their time dreaming of what they want to achieve. Rather, they spend their time working towards the actualisation of their dreams.' **– Tolu' A. Akinyemi**

In order for dreams to be fulfilled, there must be a fundamental change in one's outlook on life. We must go beyond being dreamers to becoming action-takers.

Where do you see yourself in the near future? Do you have articulated plans to achieve those dreams? In life, we need more than dreams and more than grandiose vision to be successful. We need to get our hands dirty, have a plan, and put the plan to work.

I have dreams of earning seven-digit figures from my book sales. But dreaming alone won't make this happen. First, the books must be written. Then I must have a clear, concise, and creative marketing strategy to make the sales that I want.

I had dreams in the past that someday I will be a bestselling, award-winning author. They're both a reality, today. But I wasn't just wishing for it. I put the effort into being a writer: reading, learning, and making time to write despite having a full-time job.

Achieving anything worthwhile isn't just about sowing positive words. It's not just about believing in yourself. Yes, those are very important, but they must be followed by attendant actions. The greatest proof that you believe in yourself is that you take action. No words of affirmation will come to pass if you don't act.

Dreams and visions without concrete steps are nothing but an illusion.

As a mentor in a high school in Cheshunt, I asked a Year 10 student why he wanted to pursue higher education. He answered, "I want to live in a big house and drive the latest-model car in town." That's not a bad dream, but having an education is not enough to guarantee having the niceties of life. My mentee was on the right track by envisioning the future he wanted, even though his motivation is too ephemeral. I won't be dwelling on that.

With this vision of the future, the next step is to ensure that he takes action towards making them come true. Wishful thinking won't do. Dreaming about big houses and fast cars won't make this happen. He will need more than dreams to make his dream come true.

In this day and age of the social media generation, where people practically spend their lives on various social media channels, it's quite easy to get lost in the make-believe world of content creators, where everything is beautifully curated and filtered to sway and impress a gullible audience.

If your goal is to achieve success like your role models on those social platforms, your phone must not be glued to your palm all day. Go offline and do the work. Imagine a world where Lionel Messi and Cristiano Ronaldo wile away their time at parties and on social media instead of putting in the work on the training ground. We wouldn't be debating which of them is the G.O.A.T (Greatest of All Time), for they would be nothing but average, inconsequential football players. These two champions are talented. Yes, they both have dreams of being the best. But they didn't just dream of success. They also applied themselves to their dream of conquering their sport. When their teammates are questioned about them, you hear them talking about how Messi and Ronaldo are always the first to arrive at training and the last to leave. The truth is, the fulfilment of vision is hard work!

Tennis stars Novak Djokovic, Roger Federer, Rafael Nadal, and the Williams sisters were not just dreamers. They were exemplary athletes who applied themselves on the training field. And this is why they were winners of multiple Grand Slams and other competitions.

With the rise of Afrobeats, a lot of young boys and girls, especially in Africa, want to be the next star, like Davido and Wizkid; but for many, these dreams will only remain dreams because they don't have the discipline to make themselves superstars.

My message in this chapter is that dreaming is not a magic wand that will make you become an overnight success. Dreaming alone doesn't give birth to solutions, and it doesn't put food on the table. So, after you've dreamed and written down your vision, take it a step further and put in the work.

Be deliberate about turning your dreams into reality. By being deliberate, you'll shun time-wasting activities. Intentionality means you're taking concrete steps to turn those dreams into a reality. The world is full of distractions. We no longer need friends to bring the latest gossip piece in town to us. Our small and big screens do that job perfectly well for us, already. Twitter trends can keep us busy for days. The rumour mill on Facebook and Instagram is enough distraction to make even the most disciplined falter.

These distractions are sapping you of energy to invest in making your dreams come true.

******

I've made irrational decisions whose outcomes hurt me. There are some I still regret, every time I remember them. As a publisher, I've had cause to make business decisions that I would later reverse. I have taken steps that many would have seen as ludicrous — like relocating from the United Kingdom to my country of birth, Nigeria, many years ago. And, when I moved back after fifteen months in Nigeria, I needed much more than dreams to make my second coming a success. On the surface, people could have attributed my success to luck and good fortune, but behind the scenes, it took much more than that to be where I am today. I worked.

It's not often that we rip apart a working system because we want to try a new one. When the small, actionable steps of the last year that have worked for me were being reversed because of dreams with no roots, I traced my steps backwards and returned to what does work.

To achieve our dreams, we have to be ready to serve and start from a low point. But even when you're serving at your lowest point, you have to do it with class and dignity.

Many young people no longer see the dignity in labour. They don't want to serve, learn, or start from the bottom. They just want to lead; to be in the limelight from the get-go. And this is why we have a leadership crisis today and why we have start-ups crumbling at the hands of inexperienced managers who have skipped the learning and service phase which are important for the actualisation of their dreams.

******

Many people do not know this, but my alias, *Toludo* (which later metamorphosed into *Tolutoludo*), was given to me by a colleague during my visit to the Central Bank of Nigeria Abuja over a decade ago. She touted me as a future governor of the Central Bank of Nigeria (CBN). This was during the Charles Soludo administration—hence, *Toludo.*

However, those were dreams in the days when I was a student of economics, with the potential to apply my knowledge to banking and economic policy development. It would be foolhardy for me to keep nursing this ambition now, when I haven't shown enough desire and application in this field. Presently, with my expertise in financial crime compliance, combating fraud, money laundering, and terrorist activities, I can pursue any opportunity that comes up because these are my areas of interest.

Being able to apply critical thinking would do us a lot of good when evaluating our decisions in life. Beyond emotions, we need to ask critical questions when making important decisions.

These are some important questions to ask when deciding on dreams to pursue:

Are these dreams practicable?

When the fleeting emotions that trigger the dreams evaporate and we apply critical thinking, can we honestly say that the dream of winning the lottery will ever happen in our lifetime? Is this a valid dream, or an avenue for sinking hard-earned cash into a wasteful venture? Many people are addicted to gambling because they have been negatively influenced and have wired themselves to believe that, someday, they will win the lottery. The dreams last for a lifetime but the sinking hole, which is a pile of debt, has no end.

Evaluating our dreams from time to time will help us determine if we could achieve them either in the short term or in the long term. Also, irrational dreams should be discarded, to avoid wasting precious time chasing the wind.

Critically evaluating the practicality of our dreams would also aid in redirecting us when we make misplaced steps or decisions. And it would help us avoid living in a bubble far from the realities of real life.

Do I have the capacity to manage my dreams?

As a writer who went from being an unknown writer to becoming a multiple award-winning author of many bestselling books, the accomplishments on my writing journey are not just a function of mere dreams. I built the capacity for achieving them. Capacity-building means that you're able to develop yourself to become a person of immense value. Coaching people, delivering lectures, and speaking at events means that you have something to talk about. I get paid, because of my talent, to perform at events because I have built capacity over the years.

Even when your dreams are actualised, capacity-building must be continuous, if you want to sustain them. We must always hunger and thirst for knowledge. Many times, we want to birth dreams we cannot actualise or sustain.

This is, indeed, food for thought. Many people want to be the President and Commander-In-Chief when they could have been better off as councillors, mayors, or state governors.

Invest in capacity-building so that your dreams do not end up as a pile of rubble due to a lack of capacity.

Am I living in a bubble?

A dreamer lives in a bubble when dreams are not achievable. Dreaming without applying logic to them means that one is living in a web of delusion. And it's always hard when life's reality strikes.

Your dreams will make you lonely, because not everyone will see what you're seeing. It's left to you to live and die for your dream—and, by all means, you should.

However, there are times when you need to ask yourself whether you're living in a bubble. This isn't because people don't believe in your dreams, but because you want to make sure that your dreams are achievable, given the resources and opportunities at your disposal. For example: it's not far-reaching for Lionel Messi to dream of being a 100-metre race champion, but how feasible is this dream?

Am I living in a bubble? Where will this road lead me to? Will these dreams ever become actualised, or will they forever remain in the realm of imagination? These are questions that can help us ensure that our lives are not perpetually lived in a bubble.

As an example, I hear, from time to time, that many authors do not sell even one hundred books in their lifetime, yet a new author dreams of becoming a full-time writer. That would amount to insanity if there were no clear strategy to make a success of this aspiration.

It's easy to become stuck in the bubble of one's dream, so we must always carry out a constant evaluation, as a form of reality check.

******

I have seen enough of life to know that the road to success is not paved with gold. To achieve success, dreaming won't turn your wishful thinking into reality. Get into the mud. Build capacity. Develop yourself. Be ready in the place of preparation. Disconnect from the *bubble trap*. Dreams that depend on luck and sheer fortune are nothing but delusions.

CHAPTER 5

FAILURE HURTS

'Even if your life is smooth sailing and you have not experienced failures or loss, always have it on your mind that failing and falling is part of the human experience.' – **Tolu' A. Akinyemi**

Anyone who is genuinely making an effort to make the most of their life will experience failure at many points. It hurts, but some of us have learned to wear our failures like a badge of honour.

While failure is often a result of situations beyond our control, we often fail because we didn't put in the right effort. As an undergraduate, I wasn't comfortable graduating with a second-class lower division. I knew I had the brains to graduate with, at worst, a second class upper, if I had put in the work. But my attention was divided throughout my undergraduate studies and my final grade reflected my overall investment in that process. My harvest was a result of the seeds I had sown.

Failure can affect one's perspectives in life. Some fear starting something new because they're afraid that they will fail, while some failed and couldn't start all over again because they lacked the inner will, grit, and even external motivation to do so. Failure has stopped many people from fulfilling their potential. But we can't avoid failure, so we have to develop the right mentality to overcome it.

I was a partner in a business, some decades ago. And, despite all the efforts and resources I put into the business, it failed. To this day, the failure of the business still hurts, but it didn't stop me from taking new business risks again. The failure became a propeller instead of a limiting factor.

There is always the possibility of failing in a project, dream, or plan. However, if we experience this failure, it should not define our lives.

Fail, but fail in the right direction. Failures are inevitable, but learning from them will save us from future pitfalls.

I have heard people say that it's better to learn from other people's experiences rather than ours. But if it takes a crushing defeat like the one Anthony Joshua suffered in the hands of

Andy Ruiz Jr., to learn how to win, then that failure has served a good purpose.

When Anthony Joshua lost the boxing bout to Andy Ruiz Jr., that failure probably hurt him badly. Everyone had an opinion about him. Some said he was finished, but he never let his guard down. Instead, he went back to the gym, learned from his first mistakes, and bounced back with a victory. Champions are forged in the fire of adversity.

The failure hurts, but he didn't hold pity parties, sob stories, or blame games. His total focus was on regaining his belt, which he was able to accomplish. That experience was a bitter pill, but being a champion comes with both victory and defeat. Developing the right mindset in the face of adversity is a trait of champions. He prepared for the rematch as if his life depended on it. In truth, his boxing career depended on this, and he came out with all guns blazing and won the rematch.

Many businesses have had to shut down because of the Coronavirus pandemic. The failure of losing investments, money, and other assets bites very hard, but don't be too hard on yourself. It was beyond your control. Know when certain things are beyond your control and stop beating yourself up because of this. This attitude will dampen your spirit instead of helping you gather the strength to recover from failure.

Like Anthony Joshua and many others who have failed, there will be voices in our heads that keep reminding us of our failures and that keep preying on our self-confidence, telling us we're not good enough. But we should never give in to these voices. We should never give in to failure.

How do we overcome the fear of failure?

It is human to be scared of failure. After all, no one wants to fail. But, we must accept the inevitability of failure. Accepting that inevitability helps us change our mindset towards it. Though we pray against it, we prepare for it. And when it happens, we learn from it.

Learn from your failures. Be open-minded about your failings. What mistakes did you make on your journey? Are you willing to correct those mistakes? Being defensive and playing the victim isn't a tactic that will help you overcome your failures or make a headway in life. To overcome them, we need to confront our fears head-on and admit the mistakes we made. As humans, we are not infallible.

Recently, a Nigerian gospel minister was accused of impregnating a lady while on tour in the United States of America. Through his actions, he has failed his wife, Christendom, and the gospel of Christ that he propagates. This is a failure that will haunt him for a long time, even as he took the honourable step to withdraw himself from all ministration endeavours.

Even when we take steps to correct our failures, we are liable to fail again and again when we lose our guard. Anthony Joshua regained his belt from Andy Ruiz Jr., but he then lost it to Oleksandr Usyk.

The Nigerian gospel minister is now seen as a vulnerable minister of the gospel who cannot control his sexual drive or honour his vows to his wife. Failing changes how people perceive us. When we are coasting home to victories, people love us. We get the praises, endorsement deals, and the honour that is accorded to winners. However, when we fail, others' perceptions change immediately.

A recent example: at the 2022 African Cup of Nations, the Super Eagles of Nigeria were the only team to win all their group games, and they were tagged as one of the favourites to win the competition. However, they failed in the second round of the competition, losing to the Carthage Eagles of Tunisia. That was a disappointing loss, as the Tunisian team had many players out because of the coronavirus disease. This failure was hard to swallow for many Nigerian fans, and they turned on the players who had previously been celebrated earlier in the tournament.

That's what failure does to us — one minute we are being celebrated, and the next we're being disparaged.

A lot of footballers get trolled when they make mistakes. People tend to forget that these people are humans with emotions whose mental health could be affected when they are taunted.

If your failure hurts you to the point of hopelessness, seek help. Speak to someone, don't suffer in silence. I had a friend whose work permit had been revoked. At that point, he was no longer talking to me and was holding a grudge. But when he spoke out and asked for help, I was able to assist and support him towards getting a new work permit, and his situation was resolved.

******

Life is a long arc. Your failures don't determine how and where you'll end up in life. Never give up on yourself. That I graduated with a second-class lower was not the end of the world for me. In my postgraduate studies at the University of Hertfordshire, I had a commendation grade in Accounting and Financial Management. My initial failure to graduate with a second-class upper degree didn't affect me in my pursuit of excellence. It has also not affected my career trajectory. I've had a stellar career, to date.

As enunciated above, failure hurts, and can shake us to our bones. It also leaves us vulnerable to attacks. Many people have opinions that can sting and hurt our emotions, but giving up is not an option. Don't let your failure make you give up on yourself.

****

While working at a global investment bank a few years ago, they were laying some contractors off, and my name was added to the list. As the news hit home, I was shattered. This was an unexpected outcome for me, as I was one of the best-performing members of my team. My initial disappointment soon gave way to renewed hope. In the weeks that followed, I got another job in a retail bank in northwest England and was also offered a new role at the Global Investment Bank in London, with more pay and juicy add-ons.

When some colleagues called me to complain about the situation, I never saw it as a setback. I didn't complain because I had an understanding that this situation did not have the power to define my career journey. I could have opted to play the victim, have pity parties and let people commiserate with me because I lost my job. In my life, I have encountered greater issues that I surmounted. Losing a job was the last thing that could deter me from my pursuit of excellence.

The initial failure was losing a job which did not define me at that point, and the outcome was greater than I could ever imagine. I was lodged in five-star hotels in the City of London for over six months, with all expenses paid and travel costs reimbursed. It's not every time that you fail or get such bad news that you cry and become helpless and bitter. Amid your failure, give thanks; have renewed hope and believe in yourself. Learn from the experience and give it another try.

******

We have all failed at some point in our lives. And if you have not failed before in your endeavours, there is a probability that you will fail at some point in the future. Let your failures propel you to shoot for the stars. If you lose, try again. And never give up!

Let the failures push you forward and not into regression and wallowing in self-pity. Advancement after failure means the mistakes are not repeated. Having honest and open conversations is a sure way to prevent future reoccurrences. Also, evaluating why we have failed and committing ourselves to doing better would ensure that we do not make the same mistakes again.

Failure hurts. I have seen people who ended their own lives because they believed all was over for them. Therefore, it is paramount that we do not see failure as a taboo or scorn those who have failed until they become suicidal. Empathise with people, and assist them in getting back on their feet.

CHAPTER 6

WHILE MEN SLEPT

'To have a secured future, we must be willing to pay the price, in order to earn the prize.' **– Tolu' A. Akinyemi**

Many times, people see a result and covet it without knowing the process that went into achieving that result. Everyone wants to have a better life and achieve outstanding results. We all want to be the next big thing. We want to be like Wizkid, who sold out the O2 Arena for three different shows in autumn of the year 2021. But the question is, are you willing to pay the price? One of my favourite quotes is, 'To have a secured future, we must be willing to pay the price, in order to earn the prize.'

There are no fast routes or shortcuts to success. We must understand that preparation is the engine that keeps the flames of our dreams burning.

Many of us who have accomplished exceptional results have toiled while others slept. There are many distractions that can derail us from our chosen path. For you to be successful, you must be focused and single-minded in the pursuit of your goals. Achieving greatness means that you must be ready to go the extra mile to become outstanding in your field of endeavour.

As a writer, I wrote some of my books in the dead of night. But people see the results—my published books, awards, and speaking engagements—and they covet that, too, without considering the sleepless nights I spent writing them.

As of January 2022, I have published fourteen books within fifty-four months. It's not because I am super-special, but because I have taught myself the habit of getting results against all odds.

To get results, you need to develop self-denial. I once wrote a collection of poems because I didn't attend a poetry gig and the inspiration to write came to me, which resulted in a published book. That is what denial is about. There are times I want to go out and have fun or just watch Netflix, but I don't, because I have to write or invest my time in something more beneficial to my career. This is not because I don't know how to enjoy life, but because there is so much to achieve and little time to do so.

Practising self-denial is one sure way to achieve success in your endeavours. If you have exams to write, you must prepare and study. It would be detrimental to watch movies or be engrossed with social media trends, which would lead to a lack of preparation for the exams.

If you desire success, there is no magic wand that would give it to you on a silver platter. You must be awake while others are snoring away. When people commend my accomplishments and ask me to tell them how I could achieve those results, I tell them that the difference between them and those they see making strides is application.

There are far more talented writers than me who have not applied themselves to achieving success. In my career, I have sat and passed many professional certifications because I did not tarry in the place of preparation.

I'll be sharing some tips and actionable plans to help you unravel your hidden gems.

Be Deliberate About the Circle You Keep

I had a colleague whose husband used to work as a caregiver. The man, despite how smart he was, couldn't see far and beyond the present, because of the friends he kept. They were people who'd settled for what they have and who weren't putting in any effort to do better. However, when my colleague's husband changed his environment and lost touch with those friends, his life changed for good and he began to make the most of his potential. This also applies to most of us. The reason we aren't putting in the effort to make the most of our life is because of the circle we keep. We are surrounded by lackadaisical people who have settled for the less, and this attitude rubs off on us, too.

To achieve success in life, we must surround ourselves with people who can motivate us. The rule is to have people who can give you positive challenges, whose drive and passion will inspire you.

As a student of economics, I know about the opportunity cost and alternative forgone, and I apply them in my decision-making. If I spend one hour on the phone chatting with friends and another two hours surfing the web for junk news, the alternative forgone could be a few thousand words written in one of my dusty manuscripts, or tackling another unread book on my shelf.

By making it hard for people to infiltrate my circle, I can maintain a much-needed focus on achieving.

Being accessible is great. However, too much accessibility diminishes the value of a product. If you're too accessible, it becomes difficult to attract value. Being able to balance the dynamics between being overly accessible and inaccessible is a key element to achieving results. There are days when you need to shut out the noise; when you must be selfish with your time.

You can't afford to be a people pleaser if you want to achieve outstanding results in life. Learn to say 'No'. To achieve greatness, we need to set healthy boundaries, as this will ensure that we are able to focus on important things.

Being able to distinguish between urgent, important, and mundane tasks will also help us on our path to realizing noticeable accomplishments. Are you investing your energy in activities that matter to your overall growth, or are you just indulging in frivolities?

Asking these questions will help re-evaluate and re-strategize, if needed.

Keeping your circle small helps you reduce the number of sycophants and time-wasters in your life.

Live Your Life

In today's social media generation, many people are living fake lives. The social media space is a place where everything is carefully curated for gullible audiences. People show you what they want you to see. They tell you what they want you to know. For many, it's all about appealing to the emotions of people, setting trends, and being talked about as a person of influence.

To achieve results while others are being carried away by the perception of a glamorous life, do not get lost in the chase for a trendy lifestyle. Remember: to achieve outstanding results, you must sow your seeds in due season.

There are times when Facebook reminds me that a friend has posted a story, and asks for my reaction. I do not fall for this bait or social conditioning because it's okay to stay offline and breathe. Living my life means that I am results-driven and I am always inspired to achieve my dreams.

People will not remember me for the amount of my social media followers when I die, but for my great works. Hence, in living my life, I focus on these works. Let your focus be on creating great works, and not the mundane. Live your life. Don't fake it, believing that you have made it. Stop looking for validation from strangers.

Be Disciplined

We need self-control to achieve results. There are different ways to show restraint in our everyday lives. Being disciplined means you have your life rightly organised: that you're at your desk when you should be, and you're working at the appropriate time. When you discipline yourself, it means that you cannot be easily swayed or manipulated to alter the course of your life.

In listening to people who have achieved outstanding results in business, ministry, career, and many facets of life, there is a recurring theme of discipline in these success stories. As an example: in business, you're on the road to failure if you spend clients' money or shareholders' investments for your personal use. Hence, it takes self-control to run a successful business.

You want to be a successful footballer, but you are not disciplined enough to control your eating habits and train hard in the gym. It might be time to reconsider your chosen career path. Cristiano Ronaldo, even at thirty-seven years of age, is still delivering great numbers on his football pitch. He has consistently done what many footballers in his age bracket could not do because he leads a disciplined life.

Someone reading this might ask, "How do I train or control myself to ensure optimum results?"

I'd say: start by creating an environment that makes it easy for you to be disciplined. As an example, someone who is trying to stop alcohol but continues to bring alcohol into the house will someday be tempted to try just one bottle. And it won't be long before he relapses. Habits are often a function of the environment.

It is also important to set goals that are easy to achieve. Then you can increase this over time, when you have gained mastery and momentum.

Also: with self-control, it's imperative that we understand our vulnerabilities, or else we are set up to fail.

******

In recent years, I find it quite hard to sleep for eight hours. Not that I don't desire quality sleep—I do. As a matter of fact, I always celebrate with my partner anytime I'm able to sleep for eight hours.

While I have suffered in getting quality sleep time at night, the time has been used profitably, to deliver results on my writing journey and small business enterprise. I have written books while men slept. I have birthed and incubated grand dreams because I understand the need to use my time wisely.

To have a result-driven life, change your focus. Spend time with yourself. Live your life and let self-control and discipline be the principles that direct your life. There is no glory without a story, no testimony without a test, and no product without a process. To achieve the extraordinary, we must be more than ordinary, which will require an 'extra' effort. Students who desire outstanding results in their examinations must study while others are sleeping. When you invest in the process, then you get results that are commensurate with your investment.

I have seen people who rose to the top of their chosen careers because they went the extra mile to achieve outstanding results while many slept. The majority will always sleep through life and will always struggle against and envy the minority who are successful. It behoves us to stay awake in the place of preparation so we can be part of the few who achieve results while others sleep.

CHAPTER 7

LIVING A LIFE OF INSPIRATION

'We all need some form of motivation to sail through the challenges of life. But there are days motivation alone will not fix our problems.' **– Tolu' A. Akinyemi**

People are beginning to become skeptical when they hear inspirational stories, these days. They meet every attempt at motivation on social media with mockery. And, who can blame them? A lot of people seem to know the key to success, the fundamentals of a good marriage, or how to get in shape in seven days. But, how do we motivate and inspire people when our lives are at odds with what we preach?

People are becoming more aware of the superficiality of social media. What people want is people whose life and actions inspire them—not just people who write motivational words alone.

You can choose to be an inspiration to yourself and your community. Think about doing things differently. You don't need to share ten secrets of success with anyone when you haven't applied them or seen their fruits in your own life. Being a changemaker is key to living a life of inspiration. A lot of people see problems. They know a hundred and one reasons why that idea is bound to fail. But you can be different. Don't see the problems alone—find creative ways to solve the problem, and by so doing, you'll become an inspiration to others.

To be an inspiration, you must lead an intentional life. If you want your life's story to be an inspiration to others, then your choices and decisions must be made with purpose in mind.

A pessimist cannot inspire others—only an optimist can. Those who have inspired us in life have shown grit and tenacity on their journey to success. To be an inspiration, the actions and activities that are the sum of our lives must be purposeful.

The purpose of a product is the reason that product was made. The light bulb gives us light in the darkness. That's its purpose.

The journey of purpose begins with these questions: Why am I here on earth? What was I born to do?

It's easy to inspire others when you have found your purpose and are living it. Imagine if my purpose was to be a farmer, but I was doing something unrelated to it. That means I'd be failing myself and others, as I am not living within my purpose. Finding purpose means that you have found something to live and die for.

When you're living your purpose in life, everything becomes easy for you. And you're able to replicate it in others through mentorship—for mentoring is about impacting others and replicating your success stories in others.

******

Success Breeds Inspiration

When you become successful in any endeavour, your success story will inspire people to also aim for the best in their endeavours. Take Africa's richest man, Aliko Dangote, as an example. Many African entrepreneurs have seen what's possible in the world of business and entrepreneurship because they've been inspired by Dangote. That is an indication that being successful in life means that many people will want to know about you, your work ethic, and the principles that can help them on their journeys to becoming successful, too.

So, if you aim to become an inspirational figure, go all out to achieve your goals. People worldwide are looking for successful people to emulate. A lot of young people need direction in life and are easily swayed by any appearance of success, even if it's not the real deal. So, it's important that we inspire them with actual substance.

Many young people have been inspired by Hushpuppi, the Gucci Billionaire, to enter a life of crime. If we don't show young people how they can be successful without giving in to crime, they'll be swayed by the likes of Hushpuppi, who flash ill-gotten wealth.

To become a person of immense value, let your values shine. A young man in Nigeria, Tunde Onakoya, the founder of Chess in Slums Africa, is bringing young people out of the slums to a better life. He is using his platform to advance young people who were born in slums and who were likely to live their lives in the slum, if not for interventions like his.

That's what influence is about: working for the common good. Taking those children and teens off the streets means that we are more likely to have fewer people turn to crime. Empowering these children means that they will become a funnel for empowering others.

To live a life of inspiration, we need to be the change we want to see in the world. When you make mistakes, don't let your mistakes define you. Make peace with your past, and work towards redefining your legacy.

Remember Alfred Nobel, who founded the Nobel Prize to reward people who're making positive contributions in the world. He did so after seeing the condemnation that followed after he was erroneously reported dead in an explosion that killed his brother from his invention of dynamites.

Alfred Nobel decided to start anew. And now he has left a good legacy, instead of being remembered as someone who invented something destructive.

In my capacity as a leader within the Arts and Culture community in the United Kingdom, I use my platforms to showcase the under-represented in society and create opportunities for those who would not have such access. It is fulfilling to be a blessing to a lot of people and to use my position to benefit members of the literary community.

******

Being an inspirational person means that you have good character and the right attitude. It means that your life is exemplary and worthy of emulation. If the aim is to live a life of inspiration, what we do when no one is watching is very important. Do you have integrity? Can you be trusted with responsibilities? What will be the report if the moral compass turns to examine you?

Being an inspiration to others also means that you're ready to challenge yourself to go above the ordinary. What can you do differently? How can you be a change-maker? We need creative ways to solve the problems confronting our society today. If you cannot change the world, let the change begin in your home and community. Offer your service, talent, and time to help others grow.

Over time, I've discovered that being an inspirational person means I do not give people fish. Rather, I teach them how to fish. I have helped some of my protégés, friends, and family with promising talents to migrate abroad. Empowering people means that their burden is removed from you, and you're able to focus on others. Also, when you empower people, they have the capacity to empower others, which means that many more people are lifted out of poverty.

******

We all need some form of motivation in order to sail through the challenges of life. But there are days when motivation alone will not fix our problems. Through my creative talent, I have inspired many people to believe in the impossible. Even though I always tend to downplay my impact, my writing journey has been an inspiration. Like I always say: if Tolu' Akinyemi can do it, then you also can do it better, in your niche, with your distinct gifts and talents. That's the mindset of champions finding creative ways to inspire themselves and others.

I have a very demanding job; however, this has not stopped me from creating, hoping that this will inspire many around the world to also unravel their hidden gems. If a young man from Ekiti State, Southwestern Nigeria, can rise again after the fall to become an inspirational figure, then you also can rise to become a role model.

Your background is not a determinant of your aspirations. Your dreams are valid! Whatever happened in your past should not ruin your future. You can reinvent yourself; you can rewrite the script of your life.

CHAPTER 8

AWAKEN YOUR INNER LION

'He who never risks a dime never wins an ounce.' **– Tolu' A. Akinyemi**

We often become too comfortable with the status quo because we're afraid of breaking out into the unknown. We have the potential to do so, but we stay in our comfort zone because it is a more desirable place.

I remember a time over a decade ago, when I was working in the financial services sector. I kept a lid on my creative talent because I didn't want my colleagues to know that I was a writer. I felt it could affect my career negatively, and I was not ready to blow my career. But while I was thriving in my corporate career, I knew I wasn't living to my full potential.

The giant within me was asleep. But there came the moment of awareness when I realised that my creative talent isn't a barrier to me making strides in my profession. So, I embraced my creative calling and the rest, as they say, is history.

If I had kept on believing the lie that my creativity would have a negative impact on my career and not allowed myself to express it, I would have lived my whole life with latent gifts and dreams that would follow me to my grave.

Many of us end up as mediocre because we don't challenge ourselves enough. We don't allow our gifts and talents to be refined and expressed for the world to see.

I encourage you to stretch. Stretch your thinking, renew your mindset, and change your beliefs. There is something greater on the other side. I was once employed by a multinational company in Nigeria, and I knew deep down that I was made for more. There was a conviction in my spirit that I was carrying gems that are beyond that place I was at. I was made for global impact. Although I didn't know how this would materialise, I held on to those convictions.

******

Once the lion within came to life, my life began to move in the right direction.

Like the parable of talents in the Bible, we all have different talents that have been bestowed upon us. But the question is: how are you using your gifts and talents? Are you like the servant with one talent, who buried it because he received the least?

I hear people say that they have no talent. They downplay their potential and believe the false narrative that they are not good enough. And nothing can be farther from the truth. There's no one on this earth without potential. All we all need to do is to discover the potential and awaken the lion within us.

Just like the lion rules in his territory, we are meant to dominate wherever we are, with our gifts and talents. However, a lot of effort goes into awaking the lion within us. The lion within most of us is in deep slumber because we've never aroused it once in our lives.

As I write this, my mind wanders to basketball greats like Michael Jordan, Kobe Bryant, and Shaquille O'Neal, who all rose to become giants in the game.

What do these basketball greats all have in common? How did they awaken their hidden lions? What did they do differently? The answer to these questions will benefit us, also, in our life's journey.

Break Free from Limitations

Firstly, to awaken the lion within, we must be ready to break free from limitations. What limiting factors are currently hindering you from forging ahead in life? Note these problems, think, and write their possible solutions. Then, ask yourself if you have the resources to make the necessary changes. Also, set a timeline within which you want to realise these objectives. When your goals are SMART, then you're able to measure the progress as you navigate through the challenges of life.

As a Black immigrant in the United Kingdom, coaching senior business leaders on multiple occasions early on in my author career was deeply satisfying for me. I have also lived true to my alias name, *Lion of Newcastle*. In recent years, my literary footprints have ***colossus*** etched on them. How did I come from nothing to become a writer of impact?

When you awaken your inner lion, you see every challenge as another step towards your dreams. You'll need a great deal of courage, determination, and foresight in order to awaken the giant within. I'd also say: dare to plunge into the unknown.

Why do we fear the unknown? The fear of the unknown has robbed a lot of people of the magic of the moment. They've become bound to their fears and so they cannot take risks that will push them forward.

Take Risks

To unleash the giant within, we must be prepared to take risks. He who never risks a dime will never win an ounce. Dare to risk and take your chances. Many years ago, I relocated from the United Kingdom back to my home country, Nigeria. After fifteen months, I moved back again to the United Kingdom, as I had a change of mind about my initial decision. I wasn't afraid to take risks. In life, we are always faced with choices that can alter the course of our lives. I could have remained in Nigeria and accepted the relocation as my fate. But I didn't give in to circumstances.

Also, I wasn't bothered about what people would say when I made the choice, together with my partner, to move away from our comfort zones, on both occasions. Likewise, you mustn't be too concerned with what people will say. You're the captain of your own ship. No matter what you do in life, people will talk. Therefore, to unleash your full potential, you will have to ignore the naysayers.

Many business leaders and visionaries will tell you that their business success is the result of foresight. You must have foresight if you want to make the most of your potential.

What do you see: problems, or opportunities? Many times, we have one thousand and one reasons why things will not work. It costs nothing to be optimistic and see the bright side of life. Instead of focussing on the problems, see the opportunities of the situation. Nothing is too bleak without room for a splinter of light. Be solution-driven. Let the will to achieve outstanding results inspire you to excellence.

As a writer, I don't even celebrate my last literary success for very long before I start pushing myself to deliver on the next project.

To awaken the 'lion' within, you must have the mindset of a champion.

Be Fearless

Like the lion, be fearless. When the lion walks into the jungle, every other animal scampers to safety. Being fearless means that you're able to make decisions unafraid. Do you know how much you can achieve in life if you're able to act with courage and be decisive? As a writer, sharing your ideas with the world leaves you in a state of vulnerability. But, would your vulnerability hamper you from living your life. I'd say, *No*.

It's okay to be vulnerable. I have learned to take criticisms and feedback in my stride. That's part of an author's life—accepting that your work will not be loved and welcomed by everyone. This is the sad reality.

This principle can also be applied by people who want to unravel their hidden gems. Constantly reminding yourself that not everyone will see or appreciate what you bring to the table, but showing up anyway, will do you a lot of good. Courting the acceptance and approval of everyone is a recipe for disaster.

Try New Things

To awaken your inner lion, be willing to try new things. Getting stuck on old ideas hinders us from making progress.

Also, the work must match the dreams. Being a king is not just by mere pronouncements and motivational rhetoric. To awaken the giant within, have a plan of action and outline the necessary steps to achieve your goals.

Some people do not believe in goal-setting. However, goal-setting would be an invaluable attribute in order to achieve the extraordinary. For instance, If Burna Boy's goal was to win the Grammys, without a goal and a well-thought plan of action, it would remain a dream. There won't be any propelling force to drive him to achieve this goal. However, with a goal in place, he'd begin to work towards producing the outstanding music that would make him a Grammy winner. That's the benefit of setting goals.

Do not set goals that might be too difficult to achieve. Start with goals that are easily achievable, as this will inspire you to aim for the next level.

Immerse Yourself In Success Stories

To become a giant in your field of endeavour, let the success stories of those who have done what you're looking to accomplish inspire you. What have they done? How did they achieve their results? What can you learn from them and what can you do differently? Watch their videos, listen to their messages, and let the positive energy from these inspirational people inspire you to find your voice.

I have mentored a few writers whom I believe are living below their potential because they have yet to invest their time and energy into immersing themselves in the success stories of their mentors and others of his ilk. When you always want people to spoon-feed you, the potential to become a giant is very low.

Becoming immersed in success stories is not just about listening to these stories, but applying the lessons from them to your personal life. Rather than hating successful people, you can learn a thing or two from them—things that can help shape your life.

Excel Through Innovation

To reveal the giant within, excelling through innovation could help accelerate our growth. What novel ideas do you have? The world thrives on innovation.

Let creativity be the bedrock of your life. Innovating means that you always challenge yourself to birth new ideas. Even if you don't have a novel idea, can you find creative ways to locate solutions to the challenges confronting you, from pre-existing ideas?

A protégé of mine who wanted to pay for a service in pounds sterling was commissioned to deliver projects for me which he used to offset his bills. By doing that, I didn't see him as a burden, but as a young man who was willing to use his talent creatively to solve his problems.

Instead of looking for someone to burden with your responsibilities, are there ways in which you can serve? Are there innovative ideas that can impact your local communities?

Many years ago, within the estate we lived on in Lagos, Nigeria, my brother started a car wash business, helping residents wash their cars without the need to visit a car wash. A lot of residents bought into the idea, as that was a solution to a problem that many faced.

Excelling through innovating means that you're willing to challenge the status quo and excel beyond the limitations of your environment.

******

There is a giant within every one of us. We must awaken it so we can live to our full potential. Don't give in to limitations. Refuse to be confined in the conventional box. Dare to do the impossible. Don't die with your talents unexpressed.

You have fed yourself the lies long enough to where they have become your truth. The time to start believing in a new reality is now. We fail in life because we have lost the ability to believe in our capability to achieve outstanding results. There is a spark within your soul, waiting to be ignited. You're more than your present level, so step out of the shadows and walk into your awakening.

I'll close with this: if Tolu' Akinyemi can do this, then you can also do it better in your niche, with your distinct gifts.

CHAPTER 9

SUCCESS WITHOUT CUTTING CORNERS

'When we all work towards a common goal, we can achieve a lot together.' **– Tolu' A. Akinyemi**

There is an increasing need for successful people to tell young people their stories so these youths will know that there is no shortcut to success.

Many people in society today are no longer ready to toil and sweat in order to become successful. In my home country, Nigeria, many young people now embrace internet fraud (or Yahoo, as it's called). Along with this is also the threat of ritual killings. These issues show the level of decay prevalent in society today.

On the academic front, some students are no longer committed to reading and studying to achieve excellent grades on their exams. Examination malpractice has become plague that affects the quality of the graduates our universities produce.

While studying for my master's degree, some students paid to have their coursework done for them. Some pay other people to write their dissertation. People are more concerned about the result than investing in the process that will birth the result.

From the political leaders looting the treasury to organization heads fainting during cross-examination to people with unknown sources of wealth becoming role models to young people, it's evident that, as leadership values regress, the followers no longer see reasons to uphold the dignity of labour.

In the workplace, curriculum vitae fraud is on the increase. Some people either present non-existent work experiences to get jobs, or overstate their experiences. The excuse is that recruiters rarely allow inexperienced candidates to learn on the job; hence, candidates resort to private training and certifications while padding up their work experience to get jobs.

The rot in society has become so deep that no institution is immune from it. But we can create changes if we begin at a personal level, because what makes up a society or an institution are people. Once people change, societies and institutions will also change.

To tackle this rot, though, we need to evaluate what the possible solutions are.

Get Our Politics Right

Politics is what ties everything together in a society. Getting our politics right and putting the right people in leadership positions is an important step to take in tackling societal rot.

Most of the problems we have in political leadership in many countries stem from the fact that the interests of leaders override the common good. Hence, we see leaders who are looking to embezzle public funds and make laws that they are not willing to abide by, as seen in the example of Boris Johnson, the Prime Minister of the United Kingdom, and the party-gate scandal. A lot of citizens look up to political leadership, and when they see the leaders leading by example, they are motivated to do the same.

In Nigeria, politicians became overnight billionaires on account of holding political offices. As a result, when candidates aspire for public office, their motivation is to steal public funds and not to serve the people.

When service is at the heart of our politics, the state will progress. This brings up discussions regarding selflessness and the public good, which overrides selfish agendas.

Society will continue to experience corruption and rot unless service becomes the heart of our politics.

Exemplary leadership in public office would likely lead to a chain reaction as the followers' cognitive behaviours will be influenced by what they see. I have lived in both the United Kingdom and Nigeria for an extensive number of years, and I know how a positive political system can greatly increase the quality of human life and our interaction in society.

Society is left at the mercy of political bandits when good and capable people see politics as a dirty game. When we have exemplary leadership in the political space and people who are ready to lead the way, then people will aim for success without trying to circumvent the process.

Stop Glorifying Inanities

The menace of people aiming for success at all costs will continue unhindered if we have a society where we celebrate those with shady characters and unknown sources of wealth. In some instances, we elevate these unfit characters to the highest offices in our land. Hence, when people see bad people thriving, this assures them that there are no consequences for evil, and they become willing to do whatever it takes to achieve success.

Before the "Billionaire Gucci Master" Hushpuppi was arrested in the UAE, he was courted by the high and mighty in society. Politicians, celebrities, and many young people saw him as a role model because he had stupendous wealth. His source of wealth was never known, and anyone who tried to question him was trolled and tagged as a *hater*.

The celebration of the likes of Hushpuppi show what our society has become, celebrating and glorifying inanities which drive more people to cut corners to achieve success.

When we accept that flaunting wealth, quick wins, and things that do not matter are some of the issues that are affecting society, then we can begin to elevate conversations around the dignity of labour, promoting a society where people are willing to follow the process to attain success.

Tell Your Stories – The Whole Story

I believe some successful people do not tell their whole story. They tend to paint a picture-perfect life: that which they want the world to see.

In telling their success stories, they only share what they want the world to hear and know. This does not help others, who want to understand both the process and the pitfalls along the way.

As a writer, I reiterate my author story all the time, to aspiring writers, telling them about the mistakes I made on this journey and how it's perfectly okay to be vulnerable. As we all know, the art of storytelling comes with a vulnerability evident to the naked eye. When people hear more from successful people, they gain insight into what it takes to build a multi-billion empire (as an example). Some successful people hang their successes solely on the grace of God.

Can you tell us how you progressed from being a fashion designer to an oil magnate in a few years? The reason it's important to hear these stories is to inspire the upcoming generation to dare to dream. Also, telling our success stories can drastically help in setting expectations for those who aspire to become what you are.

When people hear about your rejections and failures, it gives them the resilience to forge on when they encounter the same. They'll understand that success does not happen overnight, and that there are no shortcuts to achievement.

However, it's foolish to hear the stories of successful people and, instead of learning from them, you envy them and attribute their success to luck. You're disregarding their sleepless nights, countless rejections and failures, and the whole experience that got them where they are today.

We should learn from the experience of others so that we can make informed choices. I can tell you for a fact that you would be better off learning from the experiences of others, as some experiences are better if they are not yours.

For those of us who have experienced business failures, those lessons would have been avoided if there were exemplary business leaders whose stories and process could have served as a blueprint for us.

Promote a Culture of Meritocracy, Accountability, Transparency, and Equality

In order for a society to be progressive, meritocracy, accountability, transparency, and equality must be enshrined in its culture.

By promoting a culture of accountability, transparency, and equal opportunities, we set a precedence where the man who had no shoes from Otuoke (Bayelsa State) can dream of becoming a president, and have his dream become reality.

Also, when you're in a position of authority and you're accountable to the people you lead, you earn their trust, and your success in leadership becomes theirs, too. When we all work towards a common goal, we can achieve a lot together.

As a black migrant in the United Kingdom who aims to rise to the highest pinnacle in the financial services sector, lack of access and gate-keeping is a major issue that affects not just me, but other black professionals who are constrained by a lack of equal opportunities. When we all have equal opportunities, people won't seek to cut corners.

Promote a Value-Driven Culture

The more our civilization evolves, the more our moral cadence continues to sink to new lows. The cultural foundations that have been the mainstay of many countries are now losing relevance as Western culture continues to take root. To have a society that works for all, good values must be promoted, once again.

I was born in Ekiti State, in a south-western part of Nigeria mainly dominated by the Yoruba-speaking people. The south-western part of Nigeria has always thrived on the age-long tradition of respect for elders. But, with popular culture's rise, those values are fast fading away. The dynamics of the societies that we imitate are different from ours. But we imitate them anyway, because we lack a knowledge of history and an appreciation for our roots.

As a financial crime compliance consultant, I'm aware of the challenges that money laundering and terrorist financing and human trafficking (amongst other crimes) poses to our communities. There are real people behind these schemes—people who are trying to take advantage of weakness in the system to make quick money. That is why we need to build a society that is built on values, as only a value-driven culture can reverse the downward spiral currently plaguing humanity.

******

Whether in your career or daily life, the aim for success should be founded on a culture of integrity, accountability, and transparency. Through our actions, we must continue to show the next generation what's possible by telling our stories—the whole story. In order to create a society that works for all, equal opportunities shouldn't just be something we preach about. We must practice them in our organisations and in every societal institution.

Exemplary leadership will help to address some of the issues plaguing mankind. When leaders become great examples, we breed more leaders who are willing to go the extra mile in the service of their people. In order for people to choose the path of honour, dignity, respect, and other values that promote the 'humane' in humanity, we must continually emphasise the benefits of perseverance and endurance, working towards building a society that is fair to everyone.

CHAPTER 10

LET'S TALK ABOUT RACE

'Black is not a synonym for inferior.' **– Tolu' A. Akinyemi**

I was at my bookstand recently at the Tynemouth market when an elderly woman walked up to me and asked how I was doing, for sales. 'Great,' I replied. Continuing with a look of pity, she stated how this was a White community, with little or no Black presence. I didn't immerse myself in this garment of pity. *Being Black is not a disability.*

Racism is a prevalent issue that we must always talk about, but the colour of my skin is not a deciding factor for whether people will patronise me or not. When I attend Black Authors events and many Black writers mention that their target market is the Black community, I'm quick to mention that the bulk of my readers are White people who patronise me because they believe that my book is great, or believe it to be a great addition to their bookshelves.

I have always refused to be a *black victim*. The issues of race are ever-prevalent and cannot be downplayed. But the swansong of playing the victim because of the race card is a no-no for me. Whether you're Black or White, African or Asian, don't let your race put you at a disadvantage. Many times, we lose the will to fight even before the race starts because we have been mentally defeated. Yes, there is gate-keeping, prejudice, stereotyping, and racial abuse against ethnic minorities like me, who rarely see a role model of their ilk at the top rung, but that shouldn't be a barrier to aspiration. We must ingrain values of self-belief in ourselves.

Give it a fighting chance. Have a go at it. Don't fold your hands and say that because there is no one of my colour or race here, then I can't dare to do the impossible. You're what you say you are. And obfuscating your dreams before the race begins means that you've lost the battle even before having a shot at it.

We must amplify the need for mental emancipation within ethnic minorities. Emancipating ourselves from age-long traditions and beliefs would also help to liberate us from the shackles of limitations placed on us by our forebears. We need to liberate our minds and stop being slaves to the West. We also need to stop imitating them without regard to our cultural dynamics. Today, imitation is fast eroding our values and ensuring our spiral into the abyss at an alarming rate.

To highlight further, issues of racial injustice and inequity should continue to be enunciated. The recent coronavirus pandemic comes to mind, where the wealthier nations hoarded vaccines and the poorer nations relied mainly on donations to get their vaccination programmes going. This speaks to the widening gulf in the world today between developed, developing, and under-developed nations. And the slippery slope continues to wreak havoc on us all. To win the COVID-19 war, global solidarity would be required; not the selfishness, grandstanding and political correctness that has been the case in the past few years.

Recently, a premier league star, Kurt Zouma, had his Adidas endorsement deal cancelled and was fined £250,000 because of his irreprehensible habit of kicking his cat, which is despicable. Animal cruelty in all forms should not be condoned. However, in 2011, another premier league star, Luis Suarez, who had racially abused Patrice Evra, a left-back for Manchester United, and had also bitten Giorgio Chiellini during a 2014 world cup match and Chelsea football player, Branislav Ivanovic in 2013 during a premier league match, never had his contract rescinded by the same sports brand. Despite all his indiscretions on the football pitch with the biting and racism incidents, Adidas never ended their sponsorship deal with the player.

Meanwhile, many called for the sacking of Kurt Zouma from playing football, which led to agitations about the amplification of his offence because of his race and ethnicity. While I agree that Kurt Zouma's behaviour is abhorrent, and he was rightly called out for that, we must, however, ensure that our administration of justice isn't motivated by racism.

Do Black lives really matter?

In England, before every premier league match, players take the knee as a form of solidarity and protest against social injustice and re-echo that, indeed, there is no room for racism within football and the society at large. However, there are football players like Wilfred Zaha, who plays for Crystal Palace, who have stopped taking the knee because they believe the protest is no longer sufficient and has not reduced the issue of racial abuse that black players continue to suffer.

Global solidarity on the issue of race and equality means that we are applying the same standards to everyone, irrespective of race, colour, beliefs, or orientation. Also, when we say that Black Lives Matter, this should go beyond words of solidarity, ensuring that we back it up with actions.

One of the factors that has contributed to the unending discussion on racism is police brutality, which has caused the unjust loss of lives in Black communities.

Issues of race have dominated the discourse in the past few years because of the issue of police brutality which has led to the loss of lives within the Black Community.

While working at a consultancy firm a few years ago, I had an operations lead who kept monitoring my every move in the office. If I went to the toilet, she would complain. If I stood up from my desk to visit the toilet or get a cup of water, she would also complain about this. However, I had colleagues who would go for intermittent smoking breaks, and there were no questions asked. This leads me to believe that the issue of bias and micro-aggression should also be addressed in the workplace.

Racism will continue to be a fundamental issue when equal opportunities are not provided for all. There is a major issue of gate-keeping in many workplaces today, where only a privileged few determine who gets what role. I have seen many instances where jobs have been advertised just to fulfil audit requirements, not just handed to the anointed candidate on a silver platter. Many people from ethnic minorities also suffer from a lack of access to opportunities, hence increasing the attrition rate among these sets of employees.

Issues of race will continue to be on the front burner if reparations are not made by Western nations for the pillage and looting of resources and artefacts carried out in their former colonies. Many of these stolen artefacts are in museums all over Europe, yet these countries that would usually take the moral high ground on issues of corruption and instilling good governance and democracies around the world are not ready to do the right thing by returning what they stole in Africa. The British Museum is known to be the world's largest receiver of stolen property, with most of these stolen properties not even on display.

A quote from George Orwell's *Animal Farm* explaining disparities that exist in society still rings true, to date: "All animals are equal, but some animals are more equal than others." I have experienced, first-hand, the disparities that George Orwell's *Animal Farm* was talking about. White privilege, whether acknowledged or not, continues to be a factor in society. Every October in the United Kingdom (and February in the United States of America), we continue to celebrate Black History Month. However, I believe that the real victory will be when there is no longer a need to celebrate Black History Month or take the knee before sporting events. That would be an indication that society has truly progressed.

As long as racism exists in society, the issue of race will continue to be discussed. As touchy as issues of race are, if we don't talk about them, then the issues will continue to escalate, creating an unhealthy environment for everyone.

The Sainsbury Christmas advert of 2020, which featured a Black family, shows that racism is still a prevalent issue in the United Kingdom. The decision by Sainsbury to feature a Black family in the advert was met with racist comments and shoppers threatening to boycott the supermarket. Many people were angry because the advert featured a Black family.

That same year, an advert by Co-op featuring a Black woman was also met with racist comments online. This shows that there is still much work to do to eliminate systemic and individual racism. There is still much work to be done to uproot racism in our society.

Although modern Britain is diverse, individual and institutional racism continues to bite at the heart of our communities. In this *Animal Farm*, some animals believe they are more equal than others. And, seeing ethnic minorities showcased brings out the fangs of racism in many. I have seen vile comments from White people who said that they switch off their televisions when ethnic minorities are talking or being featured in ads.

The metropolitan police who are supposed to uphold justice have recently faced allegations of deep-rooted racism. How do we expect such a police force to rid society of racism? The police in the US are no strangers to openly racist behaviours and aggression towards Black people. The death of George Floyd Jr. and the Black Lives Matter protests around the world ring a bell of caution, that police brutality and the oppression of minority voices is still very much present.

******

We must continue to educate ourselves on the issues of race, equality, and diversity. Building a society that works for all means that there must be equal opportunities. Discrimination on the account of race and ethnicity should be eliminated. No one country can function in isolation. The United Kingdom's National Health Service is a testament to the benefits of diversity in society. If a doctor or nurse from an ethnic minority background can help to bridge the gap within the health sector, then why do people derive fun from subjecting these minority groups to vile attacks?

During the Russian invasion of Ukraine, many Africans attempting to leave the country experienced violence, segregation, and racist treatment by Ukrainian security forces and border officials. Ukrainian nationals were prioritized over Africans at every point as people tried to flee the war-torn country.

No matter your race or nationality, if faced with a life-threatening medical situation, you do not go to the emergency room asking about the race or colour of the medical personnel who would attend to you. You won't refuse to be treated because the medical personnel that are to help you are of a different race.

This is a great way to view the issues around race. Through the years, I have paid thousands of pounds sterling to the UK government, in taxes. We need to begin to see the value that many of these immigrants bring to the table.

Education on race, equality, and diversity should commence from a young age so that young people can grow up to respect and see other people as equals irrespective of their race.

Also, the perception that immigration is a bad thing should be challenged. No country can achieve anything worthwhile without taking advantage of immigration. The United Kingdom was built into what it is today through the efforts of people from diverse races and colours: legitimate taxpayers who are contributing their fair share to the economy of the country.

In order for the world to progress, we must deal with racism in all its shades.

CHAPTER 11

THE UNCERTAINTY OF LIFE

'Failing to risk means we risk to fail.' – **Tolu' A. Akinyemi**

Life is not a straight road. There are bumps and bends that make it a heck of a journey. But don't let the chaos of the world drown you or your voice. Even with the gloom and doom in the world today, you can be a change maker. You can stand for the things that matter to you. As society crumbles on all sides to popular culture, it's okay to stand up for your beliefs and to not be deterred by the mob that is always looking for others to silence. Your voice is golden and authentic. Hold your values, dear. Don't be swayed by popular opinion. Don't let the slippery slope deter you from your chosen path. It's better to stand alone than to fall with the multitude.

Amid the chaos, nurture your talent. Tolu' Akinyemi is a writer who, despite what he has achieved so far, continues to nurture his talents and that of others, too.

Rather than complaining about the problems, can they provide you with an avenue to become a solution provider? Which opportunities exist in my current location? Even before my relocation to the United Kingdom many years ago, I was an avid writer who was passionate about books. We can unravel those hidden gems irrespective of the challenges and the divergent intersections along the way.

Nobody ever said life would be easy. I have seen enough cruelty in my lifetime, which further lends credence to this assertion. We all know that good things happen to bad people and bad things to good people.

How do we measure good or bad?

A bad person today (or an assumed 'bad person', by our logic) can seek repentance and become whole again. How do we differentiate the good from the bad? Does disaster not come in many forms? They include the natural disasters that have turned our communities into ruins and the man-made calamities that have made our skies dark and our forests burning bushes. The political elites filtering the commonwealth away can also fit appropriately into the box of man-made tragedies.

Isn't it tragic, the cruelty that rocks the world today? The pain has been endured for far too long, and the weak have no more strength left in them.

Don't quiver in the face of chaos. As you read this, choose strength. Do not be deterred by it all. As you embark on this upward journey, let your every step be a catalyst for a better world that we all can be proud of.

******

The uncertainty of life can be perplexing. Many years ago, I received the shocking news that my friend and best man at my wedding had passed. My friend of many years, who was full of life, always brimming with the next big idea, and had a growing career within the banking sector, was no more. This news was gut-wrenching, and it's a sore wound that will be present for a lifetime.

That morning, he had arrived at the office just like any normal day, but complained that he felt unwell. Not long after, he collapsed and never made it to the hospital.

Life is an uncertain place. No one is sure of tomorrow. We do not have any control over our futures. But the uncertainty of life should not be an excuse to live a mediocre life. It's not a reason to fold our hands and do nothing, because we will all die someday. The fear of death should not stop you from living your best life possible.

Despite the uncertainty of life, we must take risks. We won't make much of our lives if we don't take calculated risks.

Explore the world and enjoy the adventure that life offers. Never settle for the ordinary because that is what you have been used to. Many people do not live out their full potential because they did not dare reach for more. They are happy in their comfort zones. If you never try out something new, you might spend your whole life regretting what could have been, regretting your inability to make tough decisions at the right time. Life is always about times and seasons, and once we fail to utilise the opportunities available to us at certain points in life, we might live to regret this for the rest of our lives.

I have spent my whole life taking risks, daring, and venturing into the unknown with no certainty of a positive outcome.

There are no guarantees in life. Sleeping at night and waking up in the morning is not something we should take for granted. Many go to bed at night and never wake up the next day. Treasure every moment of this transient life. Be thankful in all situations. Rather than complaining, give thanks.

Many things might hinder us from truly living our best life. Yet, the fact that air mishaps are usually fatal has not stopped people from travelling by air, nor has the prevalence of road accidents stopped people from driving or travelling by road. Our decisions in life must not be driven by fear. The fear of an unknown 'tomorrow' has left the present in jeopardy, for many.

Thoughts like, *what if I take this course of action and it doesn't work out as planned?* has led to many unfulfilled potentials and dreams that were never actualised. Living a life of fear robs us of our victory dance.

Understanding that the odds can change in your favour at any time should be enough motivation to inspire you to aim for the stars. Never downplay your ability to make something worthwhile out of your life. If the son of a Kenya immigrant, Barack Hussein Obama II, can rise to become the 44th president of the United States of America, then there is nothing stopping you. The story of Barack Obama should inspire you towards facing the uncertainty of life and spur you to greater things.

Every phase of your journey is a vital part of a jigsaw puzzle. Never despise the days of little beginnings. Many people have risen from lowly backgrounds to soaring heights in their careers. And, through hard work and persistence, you, too, can grow. Plant your seeds in due season, so you can reap a bountiful harvest.

The measure of a great life is not in the lifespan, but in the span of its impact. Live for a purpose, so as not to die for nothing.

******

If anyone tells you that there is a manual that would help you live your best life possible, they are telling a lie. It is left for you to learn as much as possible from books, mentors, and experiences, tailoring the lessons for your life so that you can make the most of it.

It's never too late to try something new—to start a new career, to fall in love after a heartbreak, or to move to a new city and start afresh. Don't let the fear of the unknown hold you back.

Many talented people are living far below their potential because they are afraid of the future. If you cannot do it without fear, why not do it afraid?

Doing it afraid means that you still make the decision, not minding the outcome. Face your uncertainty with the mindset that you'll either make the difficult decision now, or never.

When you encounter uncertainties on your journey, look for inspirational figures who have successfully navigated through the issues that you're facing. How did they do it? What were the pitfalls on their journey? Is there anything you can do differently? Learn from them. Their experience and lessons will give you a road map with which you can navigate your journey.

Challenging oneself through success stories is one way to provide the needed push and assurance to get started. If Tolu' Akinyemi can do it, you can also do it even better in your niche.

Reflecting on my life's journey, and the uncertainties I have faced at various points in my life and having courage has helped me to confront my fears when the future looked uncertain.

There were points when the future looked bleak and I had to make difficult decisions. Even though I did it afraid, I held onto my Christian faith, trusting in God for a positive outcome.

Like me, there are times you will encounter situations that will shake you to your roots, and your choices could either be confronting your fears (even if you have to do so afraid) or succumbing to defeat. But you cannot afford to give up or give in to your fears. Many of the successful people you see out there today waded through unfriendly waves and storms to get to where they are today. If they had given in to their fears, many of the success stories we see out there would never have become a reality.

The truth is that many people live in fear and are controlled by it. Those fears have hindered many from trying at all, because of the fear of failure and rejection. For others, it is the fear of what people would say if they heard about their mistakes that kept them from exploring new things. Don't let fear dominate your life and stop you from starting the journey.

I had a protégé who once faced uncertainty on an issue, and needed to try a new route. Although she didn't have all the tools available to face the uncertain future, I encouraged her to do it afraid. We had nothing to lose by starting, anyway. Rather than throwing in the towel, she followed my advice, and we had great success at the end of that endeavour.

When you're dealing with uncertainties, you don't have to see the full picture before you start. Start with what you have, and face the future with confidence.

If anyone had told me that my decision to face the uncertainties and fears that held me bound many years ago would lead me to where I am today, I would forever be indebted to them. I rose from those setbacks to become a blessing to many others along the way. That is what happens when you take that bold step.

Some young Nigerians who launched start-ups in the Fintech space entered into uncharted territories many years ago, but they have become employers of labour today. Some of those businesses are now worth billions of dollars and have attracted investors from around the world. That's what happens to you when you start with what you have. If we don't make hard decisions, we take the risk of being stagnant in life and regretting it later on. So, then, why not make those hard decisions and be satisfied with the knowledge that it's better than not trying at all? There are only two outcomes when we take tough steps: either we have something to learn from, or something to celebrate. And, if you ask me, both are better than wondering what could have happened if you'd only taken those steps.

It is time to awaken your inner lion and face your fears with boldness. It is time to roar!

AUTHOR'S NOTE

Thank you for the time you have taken to read this book. I hope you enjoyed the essays in it.

If you loved the book and have a minute to spare, I would appreciate a short review on the page or site where you bought it. I greatly appreciate your help in promoting my work. Reviews from readers like you make a huge difference in helping new readers choose a book.

Thank you!

Tolu' A. Akinyemi

AUTHOR'S BIO

Tolu' A. Akinyemi (also known as Tolutoludo & the Lion of Newcastle) is a multi-award-winning author in the genre of poetry, short stories, children's literature, and essays. His works include Dead Lions Don't Roar (poetry, 2017); Unravel Your Hidden Gems (essays, 2018); Dead Dogs Don't Bark (poetry, 2018); Dead Cats Don't Meow (poetry, 2019); Never Play Games With the Devil (poetry, 2019); Inferno of Silence (short stories, 2020); A Booktiful Love (poetry, 2020); Black ≠ Inferior (poetry, 2021); Never Marry a Writer (poetry, 2021); Everybody Don Kolomental (poetry, 2021); I Wear Self-Confidence Like a Second Skin (children's literature, 2021); I Am Not a Troublemaker (children's literature, 2021); Born in Lockdown (poetry, 2021); A God in a Human Body (poetry, 2022); If You Have To Be Anything, Be Kind (children's literature, July 2022); City of Lost Memories, (poetry, August 2022); Awaken Your Inner Lion, (essays, September 2022); You Need More Than

Dreams (poetry, forthcoming – January 2023); and The Morning Cloud is Empty (poetry, forthcoming – March 2023).

Tolu' has been endorsed by the Arts Council England as a writer of "exceptional talent."

A former headline act at Great Northern Slam, Havering Literary Festival, Crossing The Tyne Festival, and Feltonbury Arts and Music Festival, he also inspires large audiences through spoken word performances and has appeared as a keynote speaker in major forums and events. He facilitates creative writing master classes for many audiences.

His poems have appeared (or are forthcoming) in the 57th issue (Volume 15, No. 1) of the Wilderness House Literary Review; The Writers Cafe Magazine Issue 18; GN Books; Lion and Lilac; Agape Review; Continue the Voice; My Woven Poetry; Black Moon Magazine; Calla Press; and elsewhere.

His books are based on a deep reality and often reflect relationships and life, featuring people he has met in his journey as a writer. His books have inspired many people to improve their performance and/or their circumstances. Tolu' has taken his poetry to the stage, performing his written word at many events. Through his writing and these performances, he supports business leaders, other aspiring authors, and people of all ages who are interested in reading and writing. Sales of the books have allowed Tolu' donate to charity, allowing him to make a difference where he feels it's important and showing that he lives by the words he puts to page.

He is a co-founder of Lion and Lilac, a UK-based arts organisation, and sits on the board of many organisations.

Tolu' is a financial crime consultant as well as a Certified Anti-Money Laundering Specialist (CAMS) with extensive experience working with leading investment banks and consultancy firms.

He is a trained economist from Ekiti State University (formerly known as University of Ado-Ekiti (UNAD)).

He sat for his master's degree in Accounting and Financial Management at the University of Hertfordshire, Hatfield, United Kingdom.

Tolu' was a student ambassador at the University of Hertfordshire, Hatfield, representing the university in major forums and engaging with young people during various assignments.

Tolu' Akinyemi was born in Ado-Ekiti, Nigeria and lives in the United Kingdom. Tolu' is an ardent supporter of Chelsea Football Club in London.

You can connect with Tolu' on his various social media accounts:

Instagram: @ToluToludo
Facebook: facebook.com/toluaakinyemi
Twitter: @ToluAkinyemi

www.ingramcontent.com/pod-product-compliance
Lightning Source LLC
Chambersburg PA
CBHW030839200726
48285CB00007B/2487